50 Easy Spanish Recipes for Home

By: Kelly Johnson

Table of Contents

- Spanish Tortilla
- Gazpacho
- Paella
- Patatas Bravas
- Churros with Chocolate Sauce
- Gambas al Ajillo (Garlic Shrimp)
- Sangria
- Pisto (Spanish Ratatouille)
- Jamón Croquettes
- Pollo Asado (Spanish Roast Chicken)
- Pan con Tomate (Tomato Bread)
- Flan
- Ensalada Mixta (Mixed Salad)
- Pulpo a la Gallega (Galician-Style Octopus)
- Salmorejo
- Albondigas (Meatballs)
- Gambas a la Plancha (Grilled Shrimp)
- Bacalao a la Vizcaína (Basque-Style Cod)
- Tarta de Santiago (Almond Cake)
- Piquillos Rellenos de Marisco (Seafood-Stuffed Piquillo Peppers)
- Calamares a la Romana (Fried Squid Rings)
- Espinacas con Garbanzos (Spinach with Chickpeas)
- Spanish Rice (Arroz a la Española)
- Pescado a la Sal (Salt-Crusted Fish)
- Cava Sangria
- Huevos Rotos (Broken Eggs with Potatoes)
- Sopa de Ajo (Garlic Soup)
- Pimientos de Padrón (Padrón Peppers)
- Fideuà
- Sobrasada Toast with Honey
- Marmitako (Tuna and Potato Stew)
- Zarangollo (Murcian Zucchini and Egg Dish)
- Gambas en Salsa Verde (Shrimp in Green Sauce)
- Escudella i Carn d'Olla (Catalan Stew)
- Romesco Sauce

- Cordero Asado (Roast Lamb)
- Empañadas Gallegas (Galician Meat Pies)
- Berenjenas con Miel (Eggplant with Honey)
- Salpicon de Marisco (Seafood Salad)
- Carne con Tomate (Meat in Tomato Sauce)
- Crema Catalana
- Pescado a la Parilla (Grilled Fish)
- Gambas a la Catalana (Catalan-Style Shrimp)
- Espárragos a la Plancha (Grilled Asparagus)
- Tarta de Manzana (Spanish Apple Cake)
- Conejo con Alioli (Rabbit with Garlic Mayo)
- Garbanzos con Espinacas (Chickpeas with Spinach)
- Caracoles a la Andaluza (Andalusian-Style Snails)
- Pastel Vasco (Basque Cake)
- Boquerones en Vinagre (Marinated Anchovies)

Spanish Tortilla

Ingredients:

- 4 large eggs
- 4 medium-sized potatoes, peeled and thinly sliced
- 1 large onion, finely chopped
- Salt and black pepper to taste
- Olive oil for frying

Instructions:

Prep the Potatoes:
- Peel and thinly slice the potatoes. You can use a mandolin or a sharp knife for uniform slices.

Cook the Potatoes and Onions:
- In a large skillet, heat about 1/2 cup of olive oil over medium heat. Add the sliced potatoes and chopped onions. Cook until the potatoes are tender but not browned, stirring occasionally. This may take around 10-15 minutes.

Drain Excess Oil:
- Once the potatoes and onions are cooked, use a slotted spoon to remove them from the skillet, draining excess oil. Allow them to cool slightly.

Whisk the Eggs:
- In a large mixing bowl, whisk the eggs until well beaten. Season with salt and black pepper.

Combine Eggs and Potatoes/Onions:
- Gently fold the cooked potatoes and onions into the beaten eggs, making sure they are evenly coated.

Cook the Tortilla:
- In the same skillet over medium heat, add a tablespoon of olive oil. Pour the egg, potato, and onion mixture into the skillet, spreading it evenly. Cook for 3-5 minutes, lifting the edges with a spatula to let any uncooked egg flow underneath.

Flip the Tortilla:
- Once the edges are set and the bottom is golden brown, place a large plate over the skillet and carefully flip the tortilla onto the plate. Slide it

back into the skillet to cook the other side until it's fully cooked and slightly golden.

Serve:
- Once the tortilla is cooked through and has a nice golden color on both sides, transfer it to a serving plate. Allow it to cool for a few minutes before slicing into wedges.

Optional Additions:

- You can customize your Spanish Tortilla by adding other ingredients such as diced bell peppers, chorizo, or spinach.
- Serve the tortilla warm or at room temperature, often accompanied by a side of aioli or a simple salad.

Enjoy your homemade Spanish Tortilla! It's a versatile dish that works well for breakfast, brunch, or as a tapa.

Gazpacho

Ingredients:

- 6 ripe tomatoes, chopped
- 1 cucumber, peeled and chopped
- 1 bell pepper (red or green), chopped
- 1 small red onion, chopped
- 2 cloves garlic, minced
- 4 cups tomato juice
- 1/4 cup red wine vinegar
- 1/4 cup extra-virgin olive oil
- 1 teaspoon salt (adjust to taste)
- 1/2 teaspoon black pepper
- 1 teaspoon sugar (optional, to balance acidity)
- 1/2 teaspoon ground cumin (optional)
- 1/4 teaspoon cayenne pepper (optional, for some heat)
- Croutons and fresh herbs for garnish (optional)

Instructions:

Prepare the Vegetables:
- Wash and chop the tomatoes, cucumber, bell pepper, red onion, and garlic.

Blend the Vegetables:
- In a blender or food processor, combine the chopped vegetables, tomato juice, red wine vinegar, olive oil, salt, black pepper, sugar (if using), cumin (if using), and cayenne pepper (if using). Blend until smooth.

Chill the Gazpacho:
- Refrigerate the gazpacho for at least 2 hours to allow the flavors to meld and the soup to chill thoroughly.

Adjust Seasonings:
- Before serving, taste the gazpacho and adjust the seasoning if needed. Add more salt, pepper, or vinegar according to your preference.

Serve:
- Ladle the chilled gazpacho into bowls. Garnish with croutons and fresh herbs if desired.

Optional: Customize the Texture:

- Some people prefer a chunkier texture, in which case you can reserve a portion of the chopped vegetables before blending and stir them into the soup before serving.

Gazpacho is a versatile dish, and you can adjust the ingredients and seasonings to suit your taste. It's a light and healthy option, perfect for summer lunches or as a starter for a Mediterranean-themed meal. Enjoy the vibrant flavors of this classic Spanish soup!

Paella

Ingredients:

- 2 cups Spanish paella rice (Bomba or Calasparra)
- 4 cups chicken broth
- 1/2 cup dry white wine
- 1/4 cup olive oil
- 1 onion, finely chopped
- 4 cloves garlic, minced
- 1 red bell pepper, diced
- 1 yellow bell pepper, diced
- 1 tomato, grated
- 1 teaspoon smoked paprika
- 1/2 teaspoon saffron threads (optional)
- Salt and pepper to taste
- 1 pound boneless, skinless chicken thighs, cut into bite-sized pieces
- 1/2 pound rabbit or pork, cut into bite-sized pieces (optional)
- 1/2 pound Spanish chorizo, sliced
- 1 pound large shrimp, peeled and deveined
- 1 pound mussels, cleaned and debearded
- Lemon wedges for serving
- Fresh parsley, chopped, for garnish

Instructions:

Prepare Ingredients:
- Preheat the oven to 375°F (190°C). Soak the saffron threads in a tablespoon of warm water.

Cook the Chicken Broth:
- In a saucepan, bring the chicken broth to a simmer. If using saffron, add it to the broth and let it infuse.

Sauté Aromatics:
- In a large paella pan or wide, shallow skillet, heat olive oil over medium heat. Sauté the onions until translucent, then add garlic and diced bell peppers. Cook until the vegetables are softened.

Add Tomato and Spices:

- Stir in the grated tomato, smoked paprika, salt, and pepper. Cook for a couple of minutes until the tomato breaks down and the mixture is well combined.

Add Meats:
- Add the chicken, rabbit or pork (if using), and chorizo to the pan. Cook until the meats are browned.

Add Rice:
- Sprinkle the paella rice evenly over the meats and vegetables. Stir to coat the rice with the flavors.

Pour Wine and Broth:
- Pour in the white wine, followed by the hot saffron-infused chicken broth. Give it a gentle stir, making sure the rice is evenly distributed.

Arrange Seafood:
- Nestle the shrimp and mussels into the rice. Do not stir from this point forward.

Bake in the Oven:
- Transfer the paella pan to the preheated oven and bake for about 20-25 minutes or until the rice is cooked and has absorbed the liquid.

Finish on the Stovetop:
- If the rice is not fully cooked or the liquid has been absorbed before the rice is ready, you can finish the paella on the stovetop over low heat.

Garnish and Serve:
- Once the paella is done, remove it from the oven. Garnish with fresh parsley and serve with lemon wedges on the side.

Enjoy your authentic Spanish Paella, a delicious and impressive dish that brings together a medley of flavors and textures!

Patatas Bravas

Ingredients:

For the Potatoes:

- 4 large potatoes, peeled and cut into 1-inch cubes
- Olive oil for frying
- Salt to taste

For the Bravas Sauce:

- 1 can (14 ounces) diced tomatoes
- 2 tablespoons olive oil
- 2 cloves garlic, minced
- 1 teaspoon smoked paprika
- 1/2 teaspoon cayenne pepper (adjust to taste)
- Salt and black pepper to taste
- 1 teaspoon sugar (optional, to balance acidity)
- 1 tablespoon white wine vinegar

For Garnish:

- Chopped fresh parsley

Instructions:

Prepare the Potatoes:
- Peel and cut the potatoes into 1-inch cubes. Rinse them under cold water and pat them dry with a paper towel.

Fry the Potatoes:
- Heat a generous amount of olive oil in a deep fryer or a large, deep skillet over medium-high heat. Fry the potato cubes until they are golden brown and crispy. Remove with a slotted spoon and place them on a paper towel-lined plate to absorb excess oil. Season with salt while they are still hot.

Make the Bravas Sauce:

- In a saucepan, heat 2 tablespoons of olive oil over medium heat. Add minced garlic and cook until it becomes fragrant.
- Pour in the diced tomatoes, smoked paprika, cayenne pepper, salt, black pepper, sugar (if using), and white wine vinegar. Simmer the sauce for about 15-20 minutes, stirring occasionally, until it thickens.
- Use an immersion blender or transfer the sauce to a regular blender and blend until smooth. Adjust the seasoning if needed.

Serve:
- Place the crispy fried potatoes on a serving dish. Drizzle the bravas sauce over the potatoes or serve it on the side for dipping.

Garnish:
- Garnish the Patatas Bravas with chopped fresh parsley.

Patatas Bravas is typically served as a tapas dish, and it's a favorite in Spanish cuisine.

The crispy potatoes paired with the bold and spicy bravas sauce create a delicious and satisfying appetizer or side dish. Enjoy!

Churros with Chocolate Sauce

Ingredients:

For the Churros:

- 1 cup water
- 2 1/2 tablespoons white sugar
- 1/2 teaspoon salt
- 2 tablespoons vegetable oil
- 1 cup all-purpose flour
- Vegetable oil for frying

For the Cinnamon Sugar Coating:

- 1/2 cup granulated sugar
- 1 teaspoon ground cinnamon

For the Chocolate Sauce:

- 1/2 cup heavy cream
- 1 cup dark chocolate, finely chopped
- 1 tablespoon unsalted butter
- 1/2 teaspoon vanilla extract

Instructions:

Prepare the Churro Dough:
- In a saucepan, combine water, sugar, salt, and vegetable oil. Bring the mixture to a boil.
- Remove the saucepan from heat and stir in the all-purpose flour until the mixture forms a dough.
- Allow the dough to cool for a few minutes.

Fry the Churros:
- Heat vegetable oil in a deep fryer or a large, deep skillet to 375°F (190°C).
- Transfer the churro dough to a piping bag fitted with a star tip.
- Pipe 6-inch strips of dough directly into the hot oil, using scissors to cut the dough.
- Fry the churros until they are golden brown and crispy, usually for about 5-7 minutes.

- Remove the churros with a slotted spoon and place them on a paper towel-lined plate to absorb excess oil.

Coat with Cinnamon Sugar:
- In a shallow bowl, mix granulated sugar and ground cinnamon for the coating.
- Roll the warm churros in the cinnamon sugar mixture until evenly coated.

Make the Chocolate Sauce:
- In a small saucepan, heat the heavy cream over medium heat until it starts to simmer.
- Remove the saucepan from heat and add the finely chopped dark chocolate. Allow it to sit for a minute.
- Stir the chocolate and cream together until smooth. Add butter and vanilla extract, continuing to stir until well combined.

Serve:
- Arrange the cinnamon sugar-coated churros on a serving plate or in a basket.
- Serve the churros warm with the chocolate sauce on the side for dipping.

Enjoy your homemade Churros with Chocolate Sauce! This classic Spanish treat is perfect for satisfying sweet cravings and is sure to be a hit with family and friends.

Gambas al Ajillo (Garlic Shrimp)

Ingredients:

- 1 pound large shrimp, peeled and deveined
- 4 tablespoons extra-virgin olive oil
- 6 cloves garlic, thinly sliced
- 1/2 teaspoon red pepper flakes (adjust to taste)
- 1 tablespoon Spanish paprika (optional)
- Salt to taste
- 2 tablespoons dry white wine
- 2 tablespoons fresh parsley, chopped
- Crusty bread for serving

Instructions:

Prepare the Shrimp:
- Ensure that the shrimp are peeled and deveined. Pat them dry with paper towels.

Heat Olive Oil:
- In a large skillet or a shallow pan, heat the olive oil over medium heat.

Sauté Garlic and Red Pepper Flakes:
- Add the thinly sliced garlic and red pepper flakes to the heated olive oil. Sauté for 1-2 minutes until the garlic becomes fragrant, taking care not to let it brown.

Add Shrimp and Paprika:
- Add the shrimp to the pan, spreading them out in a single layer. Sprinkle with salt and Spanish paprika if using. Cook for 2-3 minutes until the shrimp start to turn pink.

Deglaze with White Wine:
- Pour the white wine over the shrimp, stirring gently. Allow the wine to reduce for another 2-3 minutes until the shrimp are fully cooked and have absorbed the flavors.

Finish with Fresh Parsley:
- Sprinkle chopped fresh parsley over the shrimp, tossing them in the pan to coat evenly.

Serve:

- Transfer the Gambas al Ajillo to a serving dish and drizzle any remaining garlic and olive oil over the top.
- Serve the garlic shrimp immediately with crusty bread on the side for soaking up the delicious sauce.

Gambas al Ajillo is best enjoyed with a side of bread to soak up the flavorful oil and garlic. It's a simple and quick dish that showcases the rich and savory flavors of Spanish cuisine. Enjoy your Garlic Shrimp!

Sangria

Ingredients:

- 1 bottle (750 ml) red wine (Spanish wine like Tempranillo or Garnacha works well)
- 1/4 cup brandy
- 2 tablespoons orange liqueur (such as triple sec or Grand Marnier)
- 2 tablespoons sugar (adjust to taste)
- 1 orange, thinly sliced
- 1 lemon, thinly sliced
- 1 lime, thinly sliced
- 1 apple, cored and diced
- 1 to 2 tablespoons fresh orange juice (optional)
- 2 cups soda water or club soda
- Ice cubes

Instructions:

Prepare the Fruits:
- Wash and slice the orange, lemon, and lime thinly. Core and dice the apple.

Mix the Sangria Base:
- In a large pitcher, combine the red wine, brandy, orange liqueur, and sugar. Stir well to dissolve the sugar.

Add Fruits:
- Add the sliced orange, lemon, lime, and diced apple to the pitcher. Mix gently.

Optional: Add Fresh Orange Juice:
- If you'd like a bit more citrus flavor, you can add 1 to 2 tablespoons of fresh orange juice to the mix.

Chill:
- Cover the pitcher and refrigerate the sangria for at least 2-4 hours, or preferably overnight. This allows the flavors to meld and the fruits to infuse into the wine.

Serve:
- Just before serving, add soda water or club soda to the sangria for a bit of fizz. Stir gently.

Add Ice:

- Pour the sangria into glasses filled with ice cubes.

Garnish:
- Garnish each glass with a slice of orange or a twist of citrus peel if desired.

Sangria is a versatile drink, and you can adjust the sweetness, fruit types, or even try white wine for different variations. It's perfect for outdoor gatherings, picnics, or any festive occasion. Enjoy your homemade Sangria responsibly!

Pisto (Spanish Ratatouille)

Ingredients:

- 1/4 cup olive oil
- 1 large onion, finely chopped
- 2 bell peppers (red and green), diced
- 2 medium zucchinis, diced
- 1 medium eggplant, diced
- 4 ripe tomatoes, peeled and chopped (or 1 can of diced tomatoes)
- 2 cloves garlic, minced
- Salt and black pepper to taste
- 1 teaspoon sugar (optional, to balance acidity)
- 4 large eggs (optional, for serving)
- Fresh parsley or basil, chopped, for garnish

Instructions:

Prepare the Vegetables:
- Wash and dice the onion, bell peppers, zucchinis, and eggplant. If using fresh tomatoes, peel and chop them. If using canned tomatoes, drain excess liquid.

Sauté Onions and Peppers:
- In a large skillet or pan, heat the olive oil over medium heat. Add the chopped onions and diced bell peppers. Sauté until the onions are translucent and the peppers have softened.

Add Zucchini and Eggplant:
- Add the diced zucchinis and eggplant to the skillet. Cook for about 8-10 minutes, or until the vegetables are tender.

Stir in Tomatoes:
- Stir in the chopped tomatoes (or canned tomatoes) and minced garlic. If using fresh tomatoes, cook until they break down and release their juices.

Season and Simmer:
- Season the mixture with salt, black pepper, and sugar (if using). Allow the mixture to simmer over low heat for about 20-25 minutes, stirring occasionally.

Optional: Add Eggs (Huevos a la Flamenca):

- Make small wells in the simmering vegetable mixture and crack an egg into each well. Cover the pan and cook until the eggs are done to your liking.

Garnish:
- Once the Pisto is ready, garnish it with fresh parsley or basil.

Serve:
- Serve Pisto as a side dish, tapa, or even as a main course. It pairs well with crusty bread or rice.

Pisto is a versatile dish, and you can adjust the vegetables and seasonings based on your preferences. It's a delicious and wholesome dish that highlights the flavors of fresh, seasonal produce. Enjoy!

Jamón Croquettes

Ingredients:

For the Bechamel:

- 1/4 cup unsalted butter
- 1/4 cup all-purpose flour
- 2 cups whole milk, warmed
- Salt and white pepper to taste
- Pinch of nutmeg (optional)
- 1 cup finely chopped cooked ham (Jamón Serrano or Jamón Ibérico)

For Assembling and Frying:

- 2 cups breadcrumbs
- 2-3 eggs, beaten
- Olive oil or vegetable oil for frying

Instructions:

Prepare the Bechamel:
- In a saucepan, melt the butter over medium heat. Add the flour and whisk continuously to form a roux. Cook for 1-2 minutes until the raw taste of the flour disappears.
- Gradually pour in the warm milk while whisking constantly to avoid lumps. Continue cooking and stirring until the mixture thickens to a smooth consistency.
- Season the bechamel with salt, white pepper, and a pinch of nutmeg if using. Stir in the finely chopped ham and cook for an additional 2-3 minutes until the ham is well incorporated.
- Remove the saucepan from heat and let the bechamel mixture cool to room temperature.

Shape the Croquettes:
- Once the bechamel has cooled, scoop out small portions and shape them into cylinders or small oval shapes using your hands. The size can vary, but a common size is about 2 inches in length.

Coat the Croquettes:

- Roll each croquette in breadcrumbs until evenly coated. Dip the coated croquette into beaten eggs and then roll it in breadcrumbs again for a double coating.

Repeat the Coating (Optional):
- For an extra crispy exterior, you can repeat the dipping in beaten eggs and breadcrumbs.

Chill:
- Place the coated croquettes on a tray and refrigerate them for at least 1-2 hours to firm up.

Fry the Croquettes:
- Heat oil in a deep fryer or a large, deep skillet to 350°F (180°C).
- Fry the croquettes in batches until they are golden brown and crispy, about 2-3 minutes per batch.
- Use a slotted spoon to remove the croquettes from the oil and place them on a paper towel-lined plate to absorb excess oil.

Serve:
- Serve the Jamón Croquettes hot, garnished with a sprinkle of salt and perhaps a side of aioli or your favorite dipping sauce.

Enjoy your homemade Jamón Croquettes as a delightful tapa or appetizer. The crispy exterior and creamy, ham-infused interior make these croquettes a favorite among Spanish cuisine enthusiasts.

Pollo Asado (Spanish Roast Chicken)

Ingredients:

For the Marinade:

- 1 whole chicken (about 4-5 pounds)
- 1/4 cup olive oil
- Juice of 2 oranges
- Juice of 1 lemon
- 4 cloves garlic, minced
- 1 tablespoon smoked paprika
- 1 teaspoon ground cumin
- 1 teaspoon dried oregano
- 1 teaspoon ground coriander
- Salt and black pepper to taste

For Roasting:

- Additional citrus slices (orange and lemon)
- Fresh herbs (rosemary or thyme sprigs)
- 1 onion, quartered

Instructions:

Prepare the Marinade:
- In a bowl, whisk together olive oil, orange juice, lemon juice, minced garlic, smoked paprika, ground cumin, dried oregano, ground coriander, salt, and black pepper.

Marinate the Chicken:
- Place the whole chicken in a large resealable plastic bag or a shallow dish. Pour the marinade over the chicken, ensuring it is well-coated. Seal the bag or cover the dish and refrigerate for at least 4 hours, or preferably overnight, to allow the flavors to penetrate the chicken.

Preheat the Oven:
- Preheat your oven to 375°F (190°C).

Remove from Refrigeration:

- Take the marinated chicken out of the refrigerator and let it come to room temperature for about 30 minutes.

Prepare the Roasting Pan:
- Place the chicken in a roasting pan. Stuff the cavity with additional citrus slices (orange and lemon), fresh herbs (rosemary or thyme sprigs), and quartered onion.

Roast the Chicken:
- Roast the chicken in the preheated oven for approximately 1 hour and 15 minutes or until the internal temperature reaches 165°F (74°C) and the skin is golden brown. Baste the chicken with the pan juices every 20-30 minutes for extra flavor and moisture.

Rest and Carve:
- Once the chicken is cooked, let it rest for about 10 minutes before carving. This allows the juices to redistribute, keeping the meat moist.

Serve:
- Carve the Pollo Asado into serving portions and serve with the roasted citrus slices and onions.

Enjoy your homemade Pollo Asado with its aromatic blend of citrus and spices. It pairs well with side dishes like roasted vegetables, potatoes, or a simple salad. This Spanish roast chicken is perfect for a family meal or a festive occasion.

Pan con Tomate (Tomato Bread)

Ingredients:

- 1 loaf of crusty bread (baguette or country-style bread)
- 2-3 ripe tomatoes
- 2 cloves garlic, peeled
- Extra-virgin olive oil
- Salt to taste

Instructions:

Prepare the Bread:
- Slice the crusty bread into thick slices or cut it into manageable pieces for serving.

Cut the Tomatoes:
- Cut the ripe tomatoes in half.

Rub the Tomatoes:
- Take one half of a tomato and rub it directly onto the surface of each bread slice. The goal is to transfer the pulp and juice of the tomato onto the bread.

Garlic Infusion:
- Peel a garlic clove and cut it in half. Rub the cut sides of the garlic directly onto the tomato-rubbed bread. The juicy tomato will help the garlic release its flavors into the bread.

Drizzle with Olive Oil:
- Drizzle extra-virgin olive oil generously over each bread slice. Use a good quality olive oil for the best flavor.

Season with Salt:
- Sprinkle a pinch of salt over each piece of bread. The salt enhances the flavors of the tomatoes and olive oil.

Optional: Toasting (Optional):
- If you prefer a warmer and slightly crispy texture, you can toast the Pan con Tomate under the broiler for a minute or two. Keep an eye on it to prevent burning.

Serve:
- Arrange the Pan con Tomate on a serving plate and serve immediately.

Pan con Tomate is a delightful and effortless dish that captures the essence of Mediterranean flavors. It's perfect as a light appetizer, snack, or as a side dish to complement various Spanish meals. Enjoy the simplicity and freshness of this classic Spanish treat!

Flan

Ingredients:

For the Caramel:

- 1 cup granulated sugar
- 2 tablespoons water

For the Flan:

- 4 large eggs
- 1 can (14 ounces) sweetened condensed milk
- 1 can (12 ounces) evaporated milk
- 1 teaspoon vanilla extract

Instructions:

Preheat the Oven:
- Preheat your oven to 350°F (175°C).

Prepare the Caramel:
- In a small saucepan, combine the granulated sugar and water over medium heat. Allow the sugar to dissolve without stirring. Swirl the pan occasionally to ensure even caramelization.
- Continue heating until the sugar turns into a golden-brown caramel. Be cautious not to burn it. Once ready, quickly pour the caramel into the bottom of a flan mold or individual ramekins, swirling to coat the bottom.

Make the Flan Mixture:
- In a large mixing bowl, whisk the eggs until well beaten. Add the sweetened condensed milk, evaporated milk, and vanilla extract. Whisk until everything is well combined.

Strain the Mixture:
- To ensure a smooth flan, you can strain the mixture through a fine mesh sieve or cheesecloth into another bowl. This helps remove any egg solids and ensures a silky texture.

Pour into the Mold:
- Carefully pour the flan mixture over the caramel in the mold or ramekins.

Bake in a Water Bath:
- Place the flan mold or ramekins in a larger baking dish. Fill the larger dish with hot water until it comes halfway up the sides of the flan mold or ramekins. This water bath helps the flan cook evenly and prevents cracking.
- Bake in the preheated oven for about 50-60 minutes, or until the flan is set. You can check for doneness by inserting a knife into the center; it should come out clean when done.

Chill:
- Allow the flan to cool to room temperature and then refrigerate for at least 4 hours, or preferably overnight, to allow it to set completely.

Serve:
- To serve, run a knife around the edge of the flan, place a serving plate on top, and invert the flan onto the plate. The caramel sauce will flow over the top.

Enjoy your homemade Flan, a classic and indulgent dessert that's sure to be a crowd-pleaser!

Ensalada Mixta (Mixed Salad)

Ingredients:

For the Salad:

- Mixed salad greens (lettuce, arugula, spinach, etc.)
- 1 large tomato, sliced
- 1 cucumber, sliced
- 1 red bell pepper, sliced
- 1 red onion, thinly sliced
- Kalamata olives, pitted
- Hard-boiled eggs, sliced (optional)
- Canned tuna or grilled chicken (optional)

For the Vinaigrette:

- 1/4 cup extra-virgin olive oil
- 2 tablespoons red wine vinegar
- 1 teaspoon Dijon mustard
- 1 clove garlic, minced
- Salt and black pepper to taste
- Fresh herbs (parsley, basil, or oregano), chopped (optional)

Instructions:

Prepare the Salad Greens:
- Wash and dry the mixed salad greens. Tear or chop them into bite-sized pieces and place them in a large salad bowl.

Add Vegetables:
- Add the sliced tomato, cucumber, red bell pepper, and thinly sliced red onion to the salad bowl.

Include Olives and Optional Ingredients:
- Scatter Kalamata olives over the salad. If you'd like to make it heartier, you can also add hard-boiled eggs, canned tuna, or grilled chicken.

Make the Vinaigrette:

- In a small bowl, whisk together the extra-virgin olive oil, red wine vinegar, Dijon mustard, minced garlic, salt, and black pepper. If desired, add chopped fresh herbs for extra flavor.

Dress the Salad:
- Pour the vinaigrette over the salad, tossing gently to coat the vegetables evenly.

Serve:
- Serve the Ensalada Mixta immediately as a side dish or add grilled proteins for a complete meal.

Ensalada Mixta is versatile, and you can customize it based on your preferences and the available seasonal produce. It's a light and nutritious option that makes a perfect side dish for various meals or a standalone salad for a quick and healthy lunch. Enjoy!

Pulpo a la Gallega (Galician-Style Octopus)

Ingredients:

- 1 octopus (about 2-3 pounds), cleaned
- 1 large onion, peeled and whole
- 2 bay leaves
- Salt for boiling water
- 4-6 medium-sized potatoes, peeled and sliced
- Extra-virgin olive oil
- Spanish smoked paprika (pimentón)
- Coarse sea salt (such as Maldon or fleur de sel)
- Fresh parsley, chopped (for garnish)

Instructions:

Prepare the Octopus:
- Clean the octopus by removing the beak and eyes. Rinse it under cold water.

Boil the Octopus:
- In a large pot, fill it with enough water to submerge the octopus. Add the whole peeled onion, bay leaves, and a generous pinch of salt.
- Bring the water to a boil. Once boiling, dip the octopus into the water three times, holding it by the head, to help curl the tentacles.
- Submerge the octopus completely in the boiling water, reduce the heat to a simmer, and cook for about 45-60 minutes or until the octopus is tender. You can check for doneness by inserting a knife into one of the tentacles; it should go through easily.

Prepare the Potatoes:
- While the octopus is cooking, boil the sliced potatoes in a separate pot of salted water until they are tender but still hold their shape. Drain and set aside.

Slice the Octopus:
- Once the octopus is cooked, remove it from the pot and let it cool slightly. Cut it into bite-sized pieces, focusing on the thicker part of the tentacles.

Assemble the Dish:
- Arrange the sliced potatoes on a serving platter or individual plates.
- Place the sliced octopus over the potatoes.

Season with Olive Oil and Paprika:
- Drizzle extra-virgin olive oil generously over the octopus and potatoes.
- Sprinkle Spanish smoked paprika (pimentón) over the dish. The amount can be adjusted according to your taste preferences.

Finish with Sea Salt and Parsley:
- Sprinkle coarse sea salt over the Pulpo a la Gallega for added flavor.
- Garnish with freshly chopped parsley.

Serve:
- Pulpo a la Gallega is typically served warm or at room temperature. Enjoy this traditional Galician delicacy!

Pulpo a la Gallega is a celebration of simple ingredients and traditional flavors. The combination of tender octopus, creamy potatoes, olive oil, and paprika creates a delightful and authentic Spanish dish.

Salmorejo

Ingredients:

- 6 large ripe tomatoes, roughly chopped
- 1 day-old baguette or country-style bread (about 200g), crust removed
- 1/2 cup extra-virgin olive oil
- 2 cloves garlic, peeled
- 1 tablespoon red wine vinegar
- Salt, to taste
- Garnish (optional): Hard-boiled eggs, jamón serrano (cured ham) or chorizo slices, and a drizzle of olive oil

Instructions:

Soak the Bread:
- Tear the day-old bread into chunks and place it in a bowl. Cover it with water and let it soak for about 10 minutes.

Blend the Ingredients:
- In a blender or food processor, combine the roughly chopped tomatoes, soaked bread (squeeze out excess water), peeled garlic cloves, and red wine vinegar. Blend until smooth.

Add Olive Oil:
- While the blender is running, gradually pour in the extra-virgin olive oil in a steady stream until the mixture is well combined and has a creamy consistency.

Season:
- Season the Salmorejo with salt to taste. Adjust the amount according to your preference.

Chill:
- Refrigerate the Salmorejo for at least 2 hours to allow it to chill and develop its flavors.

Serve:
- Before serving, give the Salmorejo a good stir. Taste and adjust the seasoning if necessary.
- Ladle the chilled Salmorejo into bowls or glasses.

Garnish (Optional):

- Optionally, garnish the Salmorejo with sliced hard-boiled eggs, jamón serrano or chorizo slices, and a drizzle of extra-virgin olive oil.

Enjoy:
- Serve the Salmorejo as a refreshing cold soup, perfect for hot summer days.

Salmorejo is not only delicious but also a versatile dish. It can be served as a starter, light meal, or even as a dip. Enjoy the vibrant flavors of this Andalusian classic!

Albondigas (Meatballs)

Ingredients:

For the Meatballs:

- 1 pound ground beef (or a mixture of beef and pork)
- 1/2 cup breadcrumbs
- 1/4 cup milk
- 1/2 onion, finely chopped
- 2 cloves garlic, minced
- 1 egg
- 1 teaspoon ground cumin
- 1 teaspoon smoked paprika
- Salt and black pepper to taste
- Fresh parsley, chopped (for garnish)

For the Tomato Sauce:

- 1 can (14 ounces) crushed tomatoes
- 1/2 onion, finely chopped
- 2 cloves garlic, minced
- 1 teaspoon dried oregano
- 1 teaspoon smoked paprika
- Salt and black pepper to taste
- 1 cup beef or vegetable broth

For Cooking:

- Olive oil for sautéing

Instructions:

Prepare the Meatball Mixture:
- In a bowl, combine the ground beef, breadcrumbs, milk, finely chopped onion, minced garlic, egg, ground cumin, smoked paprika, salt, and black pepper. Mix until well combined.

Shape the Meatballs:
- With damp hands, shape the mixture into small meatballs, about 1 inch in diameter.

Sauté the Meatballs:
- In a large skillet, heat olive oil over medium-high heat. Add the meatballs and brown them on all sides. Work in batches if needed to avoid overcrowding the pan. Once browned, transfer the meatballs to a plate.

Prepare the Tomato Sauce:
- In the same skillet, add a bit more olive oil if necessary. Sauté the finely chopped onion and minced garlic until softened.
- Stir in the crushed tomatoes, dried oregano, smoked paprika, salt, and black pepper. Cook for a few minutes.
- Pour in the beef or vegetable broth, stirring to combine. Bring the sauce to a simmer.

Simmer the Meatballs:
- Gently place the browned meatballs back into the skillet with the tomato sauce. Allow them to simmer in the sauce for about 15-20 minutes until cooked through and the flavors meld.

Adjust Seasoning:
- Taste the sauce and adjust the seasoning if necessary.

Garnish and Serve:
- Sprinkle the Albondigas with chopped fresh parsley for a burst of color and freshness.
- Serve the Albondigas hot, either as a tapa with toothpicks or as a main course over rice or with crusty bread.

Enjoy your homemade Albondigas! These Spanish meatballs are sure to be a hit with their rich flavors and comforting appeal.

Gambas a la Plancha (Grilled Shrimp)

Ingredients:

- 1 pound large shrimp, peeled and deveined
- 3 tablespoons extra-virgin olive oil
- 3 cloves garlic, minced
- Fresh parsley, chopped
- Salt and black pepper to taste
- Optional: Red pepper flakes for a bit of heat
- Lemon wedges for serving

Instructions:

Prepare the Shrimp:
- Ensure that the shrimp are peeled and deveined. Pat them dry with paper towels.

Preheat the Grill or Griddle:
- If using an outdoor grill, preheat it to medium-high heat. If using a stovetop grill pan or griddle, heat it over medium-high heat.

Season the Shrimp:
- In a bowl, toss the shrimp with olive oil, minced garlic, chopped fresh parsley, salt, black pepper, and optional red pepper flakes. Ensure the shrimp are evenly coated.

Grill the Shrimp:
- Place the seasoned shrimp on the preheated grill or griddle. Cook for 2-3 minutes on each side, or until the shrimp turn pink and opaque.

Garnish:
- Once the shrimp are cooked, transfer them to a serving plate. Garnish with additional chopped parsley.

Serve:
- Serve the Gambas a la Plancha hot, accompanied by lemon wedges for squeezing over the shrimp.

Enjoy:
- Enjoy the grilled shrimp as a tapa, appetizer, or as part of a seafood feast.

Gambas a la Plancha is a quick and delightful dish that highlights the freshness of the shrimp and the simplicity of Mediterranean flavors. It's perfect for sharing with friends and family, especially during outdoor gatherings.

Bacalao a la Vizcaína (Basque-Style Cod)

Ingredients:

- 1 pound salted cod (bacalao), soaked and desalted (see note below)
- 1/2 cup olive oil
- 1 large onion, finely chopped
- 2 cloves garlic, minced
- 2 red bell peppers, roasted, peeled, and chopped
- 1 can (14 ounces) crushed tomatoes
- 1/2 cup dry red wine
- 1 teaspoon sweet paprika
- Pinch of cayenne pepper (optional, for heat)
- Salt and black pepper to taste
- 1 tablespoon sugar (optional, to balance acidity)
- Fresh parsley, chopped (for garnish)
- Hard-boiled eggs, sliced (for garnish)

Instructions:

Prepare the Salted Cod:
- Soak the salted cod in cold water for at least 24-48 hours, changing the water several times to remove excess salt. Once desalted, pat the cod dry with paper towels and cut it into serving-size pieces.

Roast the Red Peppers:
- Preheat the oven broiler. Place the red peppers on a baking sheet and broil, turning occasionally, until the skin is charred and blistered. Remove from the oven and place the peppers in a bowl. Cover the bowl with plastic wrap and let them steam for about 15 minutes. Peel, seed, and chop the roasted red peppers.

Sauté the Onions and Garlic:
- In a large skillet or pan, heat the olive oil over medium heat. Add the finely chopped onion and sauté until it becomes translucent. Add the minced garlic and continue cooking for another minute.

Add Tomatoes and Red Wine:
- Stir in the crushed tomatoes, chopped roasted red peppers, red wine, sweet paprika, and cayenne pepper (if using). Season with salt and black pepper to taste. Add sugar if desired to balance acidity.

Simmer the Sauce:
- Allow the sauce to simmer over medium-low heat for about 15-20 minutes, or until it thickens slightly.

Cook the Cod:
- Add the desalted cod pieces to the sauce, ensuring they are well-coated. Simmer for an additional 15-20 minutes or until the cod is cooked through and flakes easily.

Garnish and Serve:
- Garnish the Bacalao a la Vizcaína with chopped fresh parsley and sliced hard-boiled eggs.
- Serve the dish hot, accompanied by crusty bread or potatoes if desired.

Enjoy your Bacalao a la Vizcaína, a hearty and flavorful dish that showcases the unique flavors of Basque cuisine!

Tarta de Santiago (Almond Cake)

Ingredients:

For the Cake:

- 1 cup unsalted butter, softened
- 1 cup granulated sugar
- 4 large eggs
- 1 teaspoon almond extract
- 2 cups almond flour
- 1 cup all-purpose flour
- 1 teaspoon baking powder

For the Topping:

- Powdered sugar, for dusting
- Santiago cross stencil or template (you can print one online or create your own)

Instructions:

Preheat the Oven:
- Preheat your oven to 350°F (175°C). Grease and flour a 9-inch (23 cm) round cake pan.

Prepare the Cake Batter:
- In a large mixing bowl, cream together the softened butter and granulated sugar until light and fluffy.
- Add the eggs one at a time, beating well after each addition. Stir in the almond extract.
- In a separate bowl, whisk together the almond flour, all-purpose flour, and baking powder.
- Gradually add the dry ingredients to the wet ingredients, mixing until well combined.

Bake the Cake:
- Pour the batter into the prepared cake pan and smooth the top.
- Bake in the preheated oven for approximately 30-40 minutes or until a toothpick inserted into the center comes out clean.

Cool the Cake:
- Allow the cake to cool in the pan for about 10 minutes before transferring it to a wire rack to cool completely.

Prepare the Topping:
- Create or find a Santiago cross stencil. Place the stencil on the cooled cake.
- Dust the powdered sugar over the stencil to create the cross pattern on the cake.

Serve:
- Once the powdered sugar topping is applied, carefully lift the stencil to reveal the Santiago cross on the Tarta de Santiago.
- Serve the cake at room temperature, and enjoy this traditional Spanish dessert.

Tarta de Santiago is not only a delightful treat but also a symbolic dessert that holds cultural significance in the region of Galicia. It's a perfect choice for those who appreciate the rich flavors of almonds and a touch of history in their desserts.

Piquillos Rellenos de Marisco (Seafood-Stuffed Piquillo Peppers)

Ingredients:

For the Seafood Filling:

- 1/2 pound mixed seafood (shrimp, crab, or a combination), cooked and chopped
- 1 small onion, finely chopped
- 2 cloves garlic, minced
- 1 tablespoon olive oil
- 1/4 cup dry white wine
- 1/2 cup heavy cream
- 1/4 cup breadcrumbs
- Salt and black pepper to taste
- Fresh parsley, chopped, for garnish

For the Piquillo Peppers:

- 1 jar (about 12 ounces) whole piquillo peppers, drained
- Olive oil for drizzling
- Salt and black pepper to taste

Instructions:

Prepare the Seafood Filling:
- In a skillet, heat olive oil over medium heat. Add the finely chopped onion and sauté until translucent. Add minced garlic and cook for an additional minute.
- Add the mixed seafood to the skillet and cook until just heated through.
- Pour in the white wine and let it simmer for a couple of minutes to reduce. Then, add the heavy cream and breadcrumbs, stirring until the mixture thickens.
- Season the seafood filling with salt and black pepper to taste. Remove from heat and let it cool.

Prepare the Piquillo Peppers:
- Carefully open each piquillo pepper and stuff them with the cooled seafood mixture.

- Place the stuffed piquillo peppers in a baking dish.

Drizzle with Olive Oil:
- Drizzle olive oil over the stuffed peppers and season with a pinch of salt and black pepper.

Bake:
- Bake in a preheated oven at 375°F (190°C) for about 15-20 minutes or until the peppers are heated through and slightly crispy on the edges.

Garnish and Serve:
- Remove the Seafood-Stuffed Piquillo Peppers from the oven and garnish with chopped fresh parsley.
- Serve the peppers warm as an appetizer or part of a tapas spread.

These Seafood-Stuffed Piquillo Peppers are not only delicious but also elegant, making them a perfect addition to your Spanish-inspired culinary repertoire. Enjoy the combination of tender seafood and the unique flavor of piquillo peppers!

Calamares a la Romana (Fried Squid Rings)

Ingredients:

- 1 pound squid tubes (cleaned and sliced into rings)
- 1 cup all-purpose flour
- 1 cup cornstarch
- 1 teaspoon baking powder
- 1 teaspoon salt
- 1/2 teaspoon black pepper
- 1 cup cold water or club soda
- Vegetable oil for frying
- Lemon wedges for serving
- Fresh parsley, chopped (optional, for garnish)

Instructions:

Prepare the Squid:
- Clean the squid tubes and cut them into rings. Pat them dry with paper towels.

Make the Batter:
- In a mixing bowl, combine the all-purpose flour, cornstarch, baking powder, salt, and black pepper.
- Gradually whisk in the cold water or club soda until you have a smooth batter. The batter should have a consistency similar to pancake batter.

Heat the Oil:
- In a deep fryer or a deep, heavy-bottomed pot, heat vegetable oil to 350°F (175°C).

Coat the Squid Rings:
- Dip the squid rings into the batter, making sure each ring is well coated.

Fry the Squid:
- Carefully drop the coated squid rings into the hot oil, a few at a time, to avoid overcrowding. Fry until they are golden brown and crispy, usually 2-3 minutes.
- Use a slotted spoon to remove the fried squid rings and place them on a plate lined with paper towels to absorb excess oil.

Repeat:
- Repeat the process until all the squid rings are fried.

Serve:
- Serve the Calamares a la Romana hot, garnished with chopped fresh parsley and accompanied by lemon wedges.

Enjoy:
- Enjoy the crispy and tender Fried Squid Rings as a delightful tapa or appetizer.

Calamares a la Romana is best enjoyed fresh and hot. The light and crispy batter paired with the tender squid create a delicious contrast of textures. Serve it with a squeeze of lemon for a burst of citrusy flavor.

Espinacas con Garbanzos (Spinach with Chickpeas)

Ingredients:

- 1 can (15 ounces) chickpeas, drained and rinsed (or about 1.5 cups cooked chickpeas)
- 1 pound fresh spinach, washed and trimmed
- 2 tablespoons olive oil
- 1 onion, finely chopped
- 2 cloves garlic, minced
- 1 teaspoon ground cumin
- 1 teaspoon paprika (smoked or sweet)
- Salt and black pepper to taste
- Pinch of red pepper flakes (optional, for heat)
- 1 cup vegetable or chicken broth
- Lemon wedges for serving

Instructions:

Prepare Chickpeas:
- If using canned chickpeas, drain and rinse them. If using dried chickpeas, cook them according to the package instructions until they are tender.

Sauté Onion and Garlic:
- In a large skillet or pan, heat olive oil over medium heat. Add the finely chopped onion and cook until it becomes translucent.
- Add minced garlic to the skillet and sauté for another minute until fragrant.

Add Spices:
- Sprinkle ground cumin and paprika over the onion and garlic. If you like a bit of heat, add a pinch of red pepper flakes. Stir well to coat the onions and garlic with the spices.

Add Chickpeas and Spinach:
- Add the chickpeas to the skillet and stir to combine with the spiced onion mixture.
- Gradually add the fresh spinach to the skillet, allowing it to wilt. You may need to add the spinach in batches if it doesn't all fit at once. Stir and cook until the spinach is wilted and cooked down.

Pour in Broth:

- Pour in the vegetable or chicken broth, stirring to combine. Allow the mixture to simmer for a few minutes until the flavors meld and the dish reaches your desired consistency.

Season:
- Season the Espinacas con Garbanzos with salt and black pepper to taste. Adjust the seasoning if necessary.

Serve:
- Serve the Espinacas con Garbanzos hot, with lemon wedges on the side.

Enjoy:
- Enjoy this flavorful and nutritious Spanish dish on its own or as a side dish. It's traditionally served with a squeeze of fresh lemon for added brightness.

Espinacas con Garbanzos is a simple and comforting dish that highlights the combination of chickpeas and spinach, making it a healthy and delicious addition to your meals.

Spanish Rice (Arroz a la Española)

Ingredients:

- 2 cups Spanish or medium-grain rice
- 1/4 cup olive oil
- 1 onion, finely chopped
- 1 bell pepper, diced
- 2 cloves garlic, minced
- 1 tomato, diced
- 1 teaspoon sweet paprika
- 1/2 teaspoon saffron threads (optional)
- 4 cups chicken or vegetable broth
- Salt and black pepper to taste
- Chopped fresh parsley for garnish (optional)
- Lemon wedges for serving

Instructions:

Prepare the Ingredients:
- Rinse the rice under cold water until the water runs clear. Drain and set aside.
- Finely chop the onion, dice the bell pepper, mince the garlic, and dice the tomato.

Sauté Vegetables:
- In a large, deep skillet or paella pan, heat the olive oil over medium heat. Add the chopped onion and sauté until it becomes translucent.
- Add the diced bell pepper and minced garlic to the skillet. Sauté for a few minutes until the vegetables are softened.

Add Rice and Spices:
- Stir in the rice, ensuring it is well-coated with the sautéed vegetables and olive oil.
- Sprinkle sweet paprika over the rice, and if using saffron threads, add them to the mixture. Stir to combine.

Pour in Broth:
- Pour in the chicken or vegetable broth, stirring gently to distribute the ingredients evenly.

Simmer:

- Bring the mixture to a boil, then reduce the heat to low. Cover the skillet and let the rice simmer for about 15-20 minutes or until the liquid is absorbed and the rice is cooked.

Fluff and Rest:
- Once the rice is cooked, fluff it with a fork to separate the grains. Cover the skillet with a clean kitchen towel and let it rest for a few minutes to allow the flavors to meld.

Season and Garnish:
- Season the Spanish Rice with salt and black pepper to taste. Garnish with chopped fresh parsley if desired.

Serve:
- Serve the Arroz a la Española hot, accompanied by lemon wedges on the side.

Enjoy this flavorful and comforting Spanish Rice as a standalone dish or as a side to complement your favorite Spanish-inspired meals. The combination of vegetables, spices, and perfectly cooked rice makes it a delicious and satisfying choice.

Pescado a la Sal (Salt-Crusted Fish)

Ingredients:

- 1 whole fish (such as sea bass or sea bream), scaled and gutted
- Coarse sea salt (about 4-5 pounds, or enough to cover the fish entirely)
- Fresh herbs (such as thyme, rosemary, or parsley)
- Lemon slices
- Olive oil for drizzling

Instructions:

Preheat the Oven:
- Preheat your oven to 400°F (200°C).

Prepare the Fish:
- Ensure the fish is cleaned, scaled, and gutted. You can leave the head and tail intact for presentation if desired.

Stuff the Fish:
- Stuff the cavity of the fish with fresh herbs and lemon slices. This will add extra flavor to the fish.

Coat with Salt:
- Spread a layer of coarse sea salt on a baking sheet, creating a bed for the fish. Place the fish on top of the salt bed.
- Generously cover the entire fish with a thick layer of coarse sea salt. Make sure the salt completely encases the fish.

Bake:
- Bake the salt-crusted fish in the preheated oven for about 25-30 minutes. The cooking time may vary depending on the size of the fish. A good rule of thumb is about 10 minutes per inch of thickness.

Check for Doneness:
- To check if the fish is done, carefully crack open the salt crust near the head or tail. The flesh should be opaque and easily flake with a fork.

Remove Salt Crust:
- Once the fish is cooked, carefully remove the salt crust. You can do this by gently tapping the crust with the back of a spoon to break it open. Brush off any excess salt.

Serve:
- Transfer the fish to a serving platter and drizzle it with olive oil.

- Serve the Salt-Crusted Fish immediately, allowing diners to enjoy the moist and flavorful fish.

Salt-Crusted Fish is a dramatic and delicious way to prepare whole fish. The salt crust not only seasons the fish but also helps to retain its moisture, resulting in a perfectly cooked and flavorful dish. Enjoy this Spanish culinary tradition at home!

Cava Sangria

Ingredients:

- 1 bottle of Cava (750 ml), chilled
- 1/2 cup brandy
- 1/4 cup orange liqueur (such as triple sec)
- 2 tablespoons sugar (adjust to taste)
- 1 orange, thinly sliced
- 1 lemon, thinly sliced
- 1 lime, thinly sliced
- 1 apple, cored and diced
- 1 cup berries (such as strawberries, blueberries, or raspberries)
- 2 cups sparkling water or club soda, chilled
- Ice cubes
- Fresh mint leaves for garnish (optional)

Instructions:

Prepare the Fruit:
- Wash and slice the orange, lemon, and lime thinly. Core and dice the apple. If using strawberries, hull and slice them.

Mix the Ingredients:
- In a large pitcher, combine the sliced fruits, diced apple, and berries.
- Add brandy, orange liqueur, and sugar to the pitcher. Stir well to dissolve the sugar.

Chill and Infuse:
- Place the pitcher in the refrigerator and let the fruit mixture chill and infuse for at least 1-2 hours, allowing the flavors to meld.

Add Cava and Sparkling Water:
- Just before serving, pour the chilled Cava into the pitcher with the infused fruit mixture.
- Add the sparkling water or club soda and gently stir to combine.

Serve:
- Fill glasses with ice cubes and pour the Cava Sangria over the ice.
- Garnish each glass with a sprig of fresh mint, if desired.

Enjoy:

- Serve the Cava Sangria immediately and enjoy this sparkling and fruity drink.

Cava Sangria is a festive and effervescent beverage that's perfect for celebrating special occasions or simply enjoying a relaxing day with friends. The combination of sparkling wine and vibrant fruits creates a refreshing and visually appealing drink that captures the essence of Spanish hospitality. Cheers!

Huevos Rotos (Broken Eggs with Potatoes)

Ingredients:

- 4 large potatoes, peeled and cut into thin, matchstick-like strips (patatas paja)
- Olive oil for frying
- Salt to taste
- 4-6 eggs
- Serrano ham or chorizo, sliced (optional)
- Fresh parsley, chopped (for garnish)

Instructions:

Prepare the Potatoes:
- Heat a generous amount of olive oil in a large skillet or frying pan over medium-high heat.
- Add the potato strips to the hot oil, making sure not to overcrowd the pan. Fry the potatoes until golden brown and crispy. This may need to be done in batches. Remove the fried potatoes and drain them on paper towels.

Season and Set Aside:
- Sprinkle the fried potatoes with salt while they are still hot. Set aside.

Fry the Eggs:
- In the same pan or a separate one, fry the eggs to your liking. For Huevos Rotos, it's common to leave the yolks runny. Season the eggs with a pinch of salt.

Assemble the Dish:
- Arrange the fried potatoes on a serving platter.
- Carefully place the fried eggs over the potatoes, allowing the runny yolks to break and mix with the potatoes.
- If desired, add slices of Serrano ham or chorizo on top for added flavor.

Garnish:
- Garnish the dish with freshly chopped parsley.

Serve:
- Serve Huevos Rotos immediately while the eggs are still hot, allowing diners to enjoy the combination of crispy potatoes and runny eggs.

Huevos Rotos is a simple yet satisfying dish that showcases the beauty of basic ingredients prepared with care. The contrast of crispy potatoes and velvety eggs makes it a delightful and comforting choice for any meal.

Sopa de Ajo (Garlic Soup)

Ingredients:

- 8 cups chicken or vegetable broth
- 6-8 cloves garlic, minced
- 2 tablespoons olive oil
- 1 teaspoon sweet paprika
- 1/2 teaspoon hot paprika (optional, for extra heat)
- 1 bay leaf
- 1/2 teaspoon ground cumin
- Salt and black pepper to taste
- 4-6 slices of day-old bread, cubed
- 4-6 eggs
- Chopped fresh parsley for garnish

Instructions:

Prepare the Broth:
- In a large pot, heat the olive oil over medium heat. Add the minced garlic and sauté until it becomes fragrant.
- Stir in the sweet paprika, hot paprika (if using), ground cumin, and bay leaf. Continue to sauté for an additional minute.
- Pour in the chicken or vegetable broth, and season with salt and black pepper to taste. Bring the broth to a simmer.

Add Bread Cubes:
- Once the broth is simmering, add the cubed day-old bread to the pot. Allow the bread to soak in the broth and soften.

Poach Eggs:
- While the bread is softening, crack the eggs into the broth, ensuring they are evenly distributed. Allow the eggs to poach in the simmering broth. You can poach the eggs to your preferred level of doneness.

Adjust Seasoning:
- Taste the broth and adjust the seasoning if necessary. Add more salt, pepper, or paprika according to your preference.

Serve:
- Ladle the Sopa de Ajo into individual bowls, making sure each serving has a poached egg.

- Garnish each bowl with chopped fresh parsley.

Enjoy:
- Serve the Garlic Soup hot and enjoy the comforting flavors of garlic-infused broth and perfectly poached eggs.

Sopa de Ajo is a simple yet hearty soup that warms the soul. It's often enjoyed as a starter or a light meal, especially during cooler weather. The combination of garlic, paprika, and poached eggs makes it a classic and timeless dish in Spanish cuisine.

Pimientos de Padrón (Padrón Peppers)

Ingredients:

- Padrón peppers (as many as desired)
- Olive oil
- Coarse sea salt

Instructions:

Prepare the Peppers:
- Rinse the Padrón peppers under cold water and pat them dry with a kitchen towel.

Heat Olive Oil:
- In a large skillet or frying pan, heat enough olive oil to cover the bottom of the pan over medium-high heat.

Sauté the Peppers:
- Once the oil is hot, add the Padrón peppers to the skillet. Allow them to cook, turning occasionally, until they blister and become charred in spots.

Season:
- Sprinkle coarse sea salt over the sautéed peppers while they are still hot. The salt enhances the flavors of the peppers.

Serve:
- Transfer the Pimientos de Padrón to a serving plate.

Enjoy:
- Serve the Padrón Peppers hot as a tapa or appetizer.

Note:

- To eat Pimientos de Padrón, simply pick up a pepper by the stem, take a bite, and enjoy the mild, smoky flavor. Remember that, occasionally, one pepper may be spicier than the others, adding a bit of surprise to the dish.

Pimientos de Padrón is a beloved dish in Spanish cuisine, often enjoyed with a glass of wine or beer. It's a simple and tasty way to showcase the unique flavor of these small green peppers.

Fideuà

Ingredients:

- 250g fideos (thin pasta noodles for Fideuà)
- 300g mixed seafood (such as shrimp, mussels, squid, and/or clams), cleaned and prepared
- 1 onion, finely chopped
- 2 cloves garlic, minced
- 1 red bell pepper, diced
- 2 ripe tomatoes, grated
- 1 teaspoon sweet paprika
- A pinch of saffron threads
- 1 liter fish or seafood stock
- 1/2 cup dry white wine
- Olive oil
- Salt and pepper to taste
- Fresh parsley, chopped, for garnish
- Lemon wedges for serving

Instructions:

In a wide, shallow pan (paellera if available) over medium heat, add a few tablespoons of olive oil.
Add the fideos to the pan and sauté until they turn golden brown, stirring constantly to ensure even browning.
Push the fideos to one side of the pan and add a bit more olive oil to the empty space. Add the chopped onion, garlic, and red bell pepper. Sauté until the vegetables are softened.
Stir in the grated tomatoes and cook for a few minutes until they release their juices.
Sprinkle the paprika and saffron threads over the ingredients in the pan. Mix well to distribute the flavors.
Pour in the white wine and let it simmer for a couple of minutes to cook off the alcohol.
Add the mixed seafood to the pan and cook briefly until they start to turn opaque.

Pour in the fish or seafood stock, season with salt and pepper to taste, and bring the mixture to a gentle simmer. Allow the fideos to absorb the flavors as they cook.
Continue simmering until the fideos are tender, and the seafood is fully cooked. If needed, add more stock to achieve the desired consistency.
Once done, remove from heat, cover the pan with a kitchen towel, and let it rest for a few minutes.
Garnish with chopped fresh parsley and serve with lemon wedges on the side.

Enjoy this delicious Fideuà with friends and family, preferably in a communal setting!

Sobrasada Toast with Honey

Ingredients:

- 4 slices of good quality bread (baguette or rustic bread works well)
- 150g sobrasada (Spanish cured sausage spread)
- Honey, for drizzling
- Fresh thyme leaves, for garnish (optional)

Instructions:

Toast the Bread:
- Toast the slices of bread until they are golden brown and crispy. You can use a toaster, oven, or a grill pan.

Spread Sobrasada:
- While the bread is still warm, spread a generous amount of sobrasada on each slice. The sobrasada should slightly melt into the warm toast.

Drizzle with Honey:
- Drizzle honey over the sobrasada-covered toast. The sweet and savory combination is key to this delicious dish, so don't be shy with the honey.

Garnish (Optional):
- If desired, sprinkle some fresh thyme leaves over the top for a subtle herbaceous flavor that complements the richness of the sobrasada.

Serve Immediately:
- Serve the sobrasada toast with honey immediately while the toast is still warm. The contrast of warm, creamy sobrasada with the sweetness of honey on crispy toast is delightful.

This Sobrasada Toast with Honey makes for a quick and flavorful appetizer or snack. It's a perfect blend of rich, spicy, and sweet flavors that will surely please your taste buds. Enjoy!

Marmitako (Tuna and Potato Stew)

Ingredients:

- 500g fresh tuna, cut into chunks
- 4 medium-sized potatoes, peeled and diced
- 1 large onion, finely chopped
- 2 red bell peppers, chopped
- 4 cloves garlic, minced
- 2 ripe tomatoes, chopped
- 1 green chili pepper (optional), sliced
- 1/4 cup olive oil
- 1 teaspoon sweet paprika
- 1 bay leaf
- 1/2 cup dry white wine
- 1 liter fish or vegetable broth
- Salt and pepper to taste
- Fresh parsley, chopped, for garnish

Instructions:

Prepare the Ingredients:
- Cut the tuna into bite-sized chunks. Peel and dice the potatoes, chop the onion, red bell peppers, and tomatoes.

Sauté Aromatics:
- In a large pot or Dutch oven, heat the olive oil over medium heat. Add the chopped onion and garlic, sautéing until they become translucent.

Add Vegetables:
- Stir in the red bell peppers, tomatoes, and green chili pepper (if using). Cook for a few minutes until the vegetables soften.

Incorporate Paprika:
- Sprinkle the sweet paprika over the vegetables and stir well to coat them evenly.

Add Tuna Chunks:
- Add the tuna chunks to the pot and gently cook for a couple of minutes until they start to brown on the edges.

Pour in Wine:

- Pour in the white wine, and let it simmer for a few minutes to cook off the alcohol.

Layer Potatoes and Bay Leaf:
- Add the diced potatoes to the pot, arranging them evenly. Tuck the bay leaf into the mixture.

Pour Broth:
- Pour in the fish or vegetable broth, making sure the potatoes are covered. Bring the stew to a gentle simmer.

Simmer Until Potatoes are Tender:
- Simmer the stew over low to medium heat until the potatoes are tender but not mushy. This should take about 20-25 minutes.

Season and Garnish:
- Season the marmitako with salt and pepper to taste. Garnish with fresh parsley.

Serve:
- Ladle the Marmitako into bowls and serve hot. It's delicious on its own or with a slice of crusty bread.

This hearty Marmitako is a traditional Basque dish that showcases the flavors of the sea with tuna and the heartiness of potatoes. Enjoy this comforting stew!

Zarangollo (Murcian Zucchini and Egg Dish)

Ingredients:

- 4 medium-sized zucchinis, thinly sliced
- 1 large onion, thinly sliced
- 4 eggs
- 2 cloves garlic, minced
- 1/4 cup extra virgin olive oil
- Salt and pepper to taste
- Fresh parsley, chopped, for garnish

Instructions:

Prepare the Vegetables:
- Thinly slice the zucchinis and onions.

Sauté Zucchini and Onion:
- In a large skillet, heat the olive oil over medium heat. Add the minced garlic, sliced zucchinis, and onions. Sauté until the vegetables are soft and golden brown, stirring occasionally. This will take about 15-20 minutes.

Season:
- Season the zucchini and onion mixture with salt and pepper to taste. Stir well to distribute the seasonings evenly.

Create Wells for Eggs:
- Make wells in the zucchini and onion mixture with a spoon. Crack an egg into each well, taking care not to break the yolk.

Cook Eggs:
- Cover the skillet and cook the eggs over medium heat until the whites are set but the yolks are still runny. If you prefer a firmer yolk, cook a bit longer.

Garnish:
- Sprinkle fresh parsley over the dish for added freshness and color.

Serve:
- Carefully transfer the zarangollo to a serving platter or individual plates. Serve it hot as a main dish or a side, accompanied by crusty bread if desired.

Zarangollo is a simple and delicious dish that highlights the flavors of fresh zucchini and eggs. It's a traditional Murcian recipe that's perfect for a light and satisfying meal. Enjoy your Zarangollo!

Gambas en Salsa Verde (Shrimp in Green Sauce)

Ingredients:

- 500g large shrimp, peeled and deveined
- 1 bunch fresh parsley, finely chopped
- 3 cloves garlic, minced
- 1/2 cup extra virgin olive oil
- 1/2 cup dry white wine
- 1/2 cup chicken or seafood broth
- 1 teaspoon flour (optional, for thickening)
- Salt and pepper to taste
- Lemon wedges, for serving
- Crusty bread, for dipping

Instructions:

Prepare the Shrimp:
- Peel and devein the shrimp, leaving the tails intact.

Make the Salsa Verde:
- In a blender or food processor, combine the chopped parsley, minced garlic, and olive oil. Blend until you have a smooth, vibrant green sauce.

Sauté Shrimp:
- Heat a large skillet or pan over medium-high heat. Add a bit of olive oil if needed. Sauté the shrimp for 2-3 minutes on each side until they turn pink. Remove them from the pan and set aside.

Prepare the Sauce:
- In the same pan, add the salsa verde and cook for 2-3 minutes, allowing the flavors to meld. If you prefer a thicker sauce, you can stir in a teaspoon of flour at this stage.

Deglaze with Wine:
- Pour in the white wine, scraping any flavorful bits from the bottom of the pan. Let it simmer for a couple of minutes to cook off the alcohol.

Add Broth:
- Pour in the chicken or seafood broth, stirring well. Allow the sauce to simmer and reduce slightly.

Combine Shrimp and Sauce:
- Return the sautéed shrimp to the pan, coating them with the green sauce. Cook for an additional 2-3 minutes until the shrimp are heated through.

Season:
- Season the dish with salt and pepper to taste. Adjust the seasoning as needed.

Serve:
- Transfer the gambas en salsa verde to a serving dish. Serve hot with lemon wedges on the side for squeezing over the shrimp. Provide crusty bread for dipping into the delicious green sauce.

Gambas en Salsa Verde is a delightful Spanish dish that highlights the freshness of shrimp and the vibrant flavors of parsley and garlic. Enjoy this flavorful seafood dish as a main course or appetizer.

Escudella i Carn d'Olla (Catalan Stew)

Ingredients:

For Carn d'Olla (Meat and Vegetable Stew):

- 500g beef brisket or chuck, in one piece
- 500g pork belly or shoulder, in one piece
- 250g Spanish chorizo
- 2 black pudding sausages (morcilla)
- 2 white pudding sausages (botifarra blanca)
- 1 large potato, peeled and diced
- 2 carrots, peeled and sliced
- 2 turnips, peeled and diced
- 1 leek, cleaned and sliced
- 1 cabbage, chopped
- Salt to taste

For Escudella (Soup):

- 1 cup rice or small pasta (like galets or small pasta shells)
- Chickpeas (cooked, from the stew)
- Broth from the Carn d'Olla
- Salt and pepper to taste

Instructions:

Prepare the Carn d'Olla:
- In a large pot, place the beef, pork, chorizo, black pudding, and white pudding. Cover with water and bring to a boil. Skim off any impurities that rise to the surface.

Simmer the Meats:
- Reduce the heat to a simmer and let the meats cook for about 1.5 to 2 hours until they are tender.

Add Vegetables:

- Add the potatoes, carrots, turnips, leeks, and cabbage to the pot. Continue simmering until the vegetables are cooked, and the flavors meld. Add salt to taste.

Prepare Escudella Soup:
- Cook rice or small pasta separately according to package instructions.

Serve:
- Remove the meats from the pot and slice them. Arrange the sliced meats and vegetables on a platter.

Prepare the Soup:
- In individual bowls, ladle the broth from the Carn d'Olla. Add a scoop of cooked rice or pasta and some cooked chickpeas.

Serve Hot:
- Serve the sliced meats and vegetables alongside the soup. Traditionally, the meats are served first, followed by the soup.

Enjoy:
- Enjoy Escudella i Carn d'Olla with crusty bread and a glass of red wine.

This Catalan stew is a festive and hearty dish, perfect for celebrating special occasions or enjoying a comforting meal with family and friends.

Romesco Sauce

Ingredients:

- 2 large red bell peppers, roasted and peeled
- 1 cup cherry tomatoes, roasted
- 1/2 cup almonds, toasted
- 3 cloves garlic, peeled
- 1/4 cup hazelnuts, toasted
- 2 slices of bread, toasted and torn into pieces
- 1/4 cup red wine vinegar
- 1/2 cup extra virgin olive oil
- 1 teaspoon smoked paprika
- Salt and pepper to taste

Instructions:

Roast the Peppers and Tomatoes:
- Preheat the oven broiler. Place the red bell peppers and cherry tomatoes on a baking sheet. Broil, turning occasionally, until the skins are charred and blistered. Transfer them to a bowl, cover with plastic wrap, and let them steam for 10 minutes. Peel, seed, and chop the peppers.

Toast the Nuts and Bread:
- In a dry skillet over medium heat, toast the almonds and hazelnuts until fragrant and golden. Toast the bread until it's crisp. Allow the nuts and bread to cool.

Prepare the Blender or Food Processor:
- In a blender or food processor, combine the roasted red peppers, cherry tomatoes, toasted almonds, hazelnuts, garlic, and torn bread.

Blend the Ingredients:
- Pulse the mixture until coarsely chopped. Then, with the blender or food processor running, gradually add the red wine vinegar and olive oil until the sauce is smooth.

Season:
- Add smoked paprika, salt, and pepper to taste. Blend again to incorporate the seasonings.

Adjust Consistency (Optional):

- If the sauce is too thick, you can add a little water, one tablespoon at a time, until you achieve the desired consistency.

Taste and Adjust:
- Taste the Romesco sauce and adjust the seasoning as needed. You can add more salt, pepper, or vinegar according to your preference.

Serve:
- Transfer the Romesco sauce to a bowl and serve at room temperature. It's a versatile sauce that goes well with grilled vegetables, roasted meats, seafood, or as a dipping sauce.

Romesco sauce is a flavorful and versatile condiment with a rich, nutty taste. Enjoy it as a dip, spread, or accompaniment to various dishes.

Cordero Asado (Roast Lamb)

Ingredients:

- 1 whole leg of lamb (about 4-5 pounds)
- 4 cloves garlic, minced
- 2 tablespoons fresh rosemary, finely chopped
- 2 tablespoons fresh thyme, finely chopped
- 1/4 cup extra virgin olive oil
- 2 tablespoons Dijon mustard
- Salt and black pepper to taste
- 1 cup dry white wine or chicken broth
- 1 lemon, sliced (for garnish)

Instructions:

Prepare the Lamb:
- Preheat your oven to 350°F (175°C).

Make the Herb Marinade:
- In a small bowl, combine the minced garlic, chopped rosemary, chopped thyme, olive oil, Dijon mustard, salt, and black pepper. Mix well to form a paste.

Marinate the Lamb:
- Place the leg of lamb in a roasting pan or dish. Rub the herb marinade all over the lamb, ensuring it's evenly coated. If possible, let it marinate in the refrigerator for at least 2 hours or overnight for enhanced flavor.

Bring to Room Temperature:
- Before roasting, allow the lamb to come to room temperature for about 30 minutes.

Preheat the Oven:
- Preheat the oven to 350°F (175°C).

Roast the Lamb:
- Place the marinated leg of lamb in the preheated oven. Roast for about 20 minutes per pound, or until the internal temperature reaches your desired level of doneness. For medium-rare, aim for an internal temperature of 145°F (63°C), and for medium, aim for 160°F (71°C).

Baste and Add Liquid:

- Every 30 minutes, baste the lamb with pan juices. If the pan becomes dry, add white wine or chicken broth to prevent burning and enhance the flavors.

Rest the Lamb:
- Once the lamb reaches your preferred level of doneness, remove it from the oven, cover it with foil, and let it rest for about 15-20 minutes. This allows the juices to redistribute, keeping the meat moist.

Carve and Serve:
- Carve the roasted lamb into slices and arrange on a serving platter. Garnish with lemon slices for a fresh touch.

Serve:
- Serve the Cordero Asado with your favorite side dishes, such as roasted vegetables, potatoes, or a fresh salad.

This Cordero Asado recipe results in a succulent and flavorful roast lamb with aromatic herbs and a golden crust. Enjoy this dish as a centerpiece for festive gatherings or special occasions.

Empañadas Gallegas (Galician Meat Pies)

Ingredients:

For the Dough:

- 4 cups all-purpose flour
- 1 cup water
- 1/2 cup olive oil
- 1 teaspoon salt

For the Filling:

- 1 pound ground beef or pork (or a combination)
- 1 large onion, finely chopped
- 2 bell peppers, finely chopped
- 3 cloves garlic, minced
- 1/2 cup tomato sauce
- 1 teaspoon sweet paprika
- Salt and black pepper to taste
- Olive oil for sautéing

Instructions:

Dough Preparation:

In a large mixing bowl, combine the flour and salt.
Gradually add water and olive oil to the flour mixture, mixing until a dough forms.
Knead the dough on a floured surface until smooth, then cover and let it rest for about 30 minutes.

Filling Preparation:

In a skillet, heat olive oil over medium heat. Add the chopped onions, bell peppers, and garlic. Sauté until the vegetables are softened.
Add the ground meat to the skillet and cook until browned.
Stir in the tomato sauce, sweet paprika, salt, and black pepper. Cook for an additional 5-7 minutes. Adjust seasoning to taste.

Assembly:

Preheat your oven to 375°F (190°C).
Divide the dough in half. Roll out one half on a floured surface to fit your baking dish.

Place the rolled-out dough in a greased baking dish, ensuring it covers the bottom and sides.

Spoon the meat filling onto the dough, spreading it evenly.

Roll out the second half of the dough and place it on top of the filling. Seal the edges by crimping with a fork or your fingers.

Optionally, brush the top with a beaten egg for a golden finish.

Baking:

Bake in the preheated oven for 30-40 minutes or until the crust is golden brown.

Allow the empanada to cool slightly before slicing.

Enjoy your homemade Empanadas Gallegas! They are delicious served warm or at room temperature, making them a perfect snack or meal for various occasions.

Berenjenas con Miel (Eggplant with Honey)

Ingredients:

- 2 medium-sized eggplants, sliced into rounds or strips
- Salt, for sweating the eggplants
- Olive oil, for frying
- Honey, for drizzling
- Sesame seeds (optional), for garnish

Instructions:

1. Preparing the Eggplants:

    Slice and Salt:
    - Cut the eggplants into rounds or strips, depending on your preference.
    - Sprinkle salt over the eggplant slices and let them sit for about 30 minutes. This helps draw out excess moisture and bitterness from the eggplants.

    Rinse and Pat Dry:
    - After 30 minutes, rinse the salted eggplant slices under cold water and pat them dry with paper towels.

2. Frying the Eggplants:

    Heat Olive Oil:
    - In a large skillet, heat enough olive oil over medium-high heat for shallow frying.

    Fry the Eggplants:
    - Fry the eggplant slices until golden brown on both sides, working in batches if necessary. This usually takes about 2-3 minutes per side.

    Drain Excess Oil:
    - Place the fried eggplant slices on a plate lined with paper towels to absorb any excess oil.

3. Assembling Berenjenas con Miel:

    Arrange on a Serving Plate:
    - Arrange the fried eggplant slices on a serving plate.

    Drizzle with Honey:

- Generously drizzle honey over the fried eggplants. The honey provides a sweet contrast to the savory flavor of the eggplants.

Garnish (Optional):
- If desired, sprinkle sesame seeds over the top for added texture and flavor.

Serve:
- Berenjenas con Miel can be served warm or at room temperature. Enjoy this delightful dish as a tapa or side dish.

This simple yet flavorful dish showcases the delicious combination of crispy fried eggplants and the sweetness of honey. It's a great addition to a tapas spread or as a unique side dish.

Salpicon de Marisco (Seafood Salad)

Ingredients:

For the Seafood:

- 1/2 pound (225g) shrimp, cooked and peeled
- 1/2 pound (225g) squid or octopus, cooked and sliced into rings or bite-sized pieces
- 1/2 pound (225g) mussels, cooked and shelled
- 1/2 pound (225g) crabmeat, cooked and flaked (optional)
- Lemon wedges for garnish

For the Salad:

- 1 cup cherry tomatoes, halved
- 1/2 red onion, finely chopped
- 1 cucumber, diced
- 1 red bell pepper, diced
- 1/4 cup fresh cilantro or parsley, chopped

For the Dressing:

- 1/4 cup extra-virgin olive oil
- 2 tablespoons red wine vinegar
- 1 garlic clove, minced
- 1 teaspoon Dijon mustard
- Salt and black pepper to taste

Instructions:

1. Prepare the Seafood:

    Cook the Seafood:
    - Boil or steam the shrimp, squid or octopus, and mussels until fully cooked. The cooking times may vary, so follow the instructions for each type of seafood.
    - If using crabmeat, ensure it is cooked and flaked.

    Cool and Prepare:
    - Allow the cooked seafood to cool completely before assembling the salad.
    - Peel and devein the shrimp, slice the squid or octopus into rings, and shell the mussels.

2. Assemble the Salad:

Combine Ingredients:
- In a large bowl, combine the cooked and prepared seafood with the cherry tomatoes, red onion, cucumber, red bell pepper, and fresh cilantro or parsley.

3. Prepare the Dressing:

Whisk the Dressing:
- In a small bowl, whisk together the olive oil, red wine vinegar, minced garlic, Dijon mustard, salt, and black pepper.

4. Finish and Serve:

Dress the Salad:
- Pour the dressing over the seafood and vegetable mixture. Gently toss to coat all ingredients evenly.

Chill and Serve:
- Refrigerate the Salpicón de Marisco for at least 30 minutes to allow the flavors to meld.

Serve:
- Serve the seafood salad chilled, garnished with lemon wedges.

Salpicón de Marisco is a delightful and vibrant dish that captures the essence of the sea. It's perfect for sharing with friends and family, especially during warm weather or as part of a festive gathering. Enjoy this refreshing seafood salad!

Carne con Tomate (Meat in Tomato Sauce)

Ingredients:

- 1.5 to 2 pounds of beef (such as chuck roast or stew meat), cut into bite-sized pieces
- 2 tablespoons olive oil
- 1 large onion, finely chopped
- 3 cloves garlic, minced
- 1 bell pepper, diced
- 1 can (14 ounces) crushed tomatoes or tomato sauce
- 1/2 cup beef broth or water
- 1 teaspoon dried oregano
- 1 teaspoon ground cumin
- 1 teaspoon paprika
- Salt and pepper, to taste
- Fresh cilantro or parsley for garnish (optional)

Instructions:

Season the beef pieces with salt and pepper.
In a large, heavy-bottomed skillet or pot, heat the olive oil over medium-high heat.
Add the seasoned beef pieces and brown them on all sides. This step adds flavor to the dish.
Once the beef is browned, remove it from the skillet and set it aside.
In the same skillet, add a bit more olive oil if needed. Add the chopped onions and sauté until they become translucent.
Add the minced garlic and diced bell pepper to the onions, and cook for an additional 2-3 minutes until the vegetables are softened.
Return the browned beef to the skillet.
Pour in the crushed tomatoes or tomato sauce and beef broth (or water).
Add the dried oregano, ground cumin, and paprika. Stir to combine.
Bring the mixture to a simmer, then reduce the heat to low, cover, and let it simmer for about 1.5 to 2 hours, or until the meat is tender. You can also cook it longer for a more flavorful result.
Check the seasoning and adjust with salt and pepper as needed.
Garnish with fresh cilantro or parsley before serving, if desired.

Serve Carne con Tomate over rice, with crusty bread, or alongside your favorite side dishes. Enjoy this delicious and comforting meat in tomato sauce!

Crema Catalana

Ingredients:

- 2 cups whole milk
- 1 cinnamon stick
- Zest of 1 orange or lemon (optional)
- 1 cup granulated sugar (divided)
- 6 large egg yolks
- 2 tablespoons cornstarch
- 1 teaspoon vanilla extract
- Extra sugar for caramelizing the top

Instructions:

In a saucepan, heat the whole milk over medium heat. Add the cinnamon stick and citrus zest, if using. Bring it to a gentle simmer, then remove from heat and let it steep for about 15-20 minutes to infuse the flavors.
In a mixing bowl, whisk together 3/4 cup of sugar, egg yolks, and cornstarch until well combined and slightly pale.
Remove the cinnamon stick and citrus zest from the infused milk, and reheat the milk until it's warm.
Gradually pour the warm milk into the egg mixture, whisking constantly to prevent the eggs from curdling.
Pour the mixture back into the saucepan and cook over medium-low heat, stirring constantly with a wooden spoon or spatula. Continue to cook until the custard thickens. This may take about 10-15 minutes. Be patient and keep stirring to avoid lumps.
Once the custard has thickened, remove it from heat and stir in the vanilla extract.
Divide the custard into individual serving dishes or ramekins. Allow them to cool to room temperature and then refrigerate for at least 2-3 hours, or until fully chilled.
Before serving, sprinkle a thin, even layer of sugar over the top of each custard. Caramelize the sugar using a kitchen torch or by placing the ramekins under a preheated broiler until the sugar turns golden brown and forms a crisp layer.
Allow the caramelized sugar to cool and harden slightly before serving.

Crema Catalana is best enjoyed chilled, with the contrast of the creamy custard and the crunchy caramelized sugar on top. It's a delightful and elegant dessert that captures the essence of Catalan cuisine.

Pescado a la Parilla (Grilled Fish)

Ingredients:

- 4 fish fillets (such as snapper, sea bass, trout, or any firm-fleshed white fish)
- 2 tablespoons olive oil
- Juice of 1-2 lemons
- 2 cloves garlic, minced
- 1 teaspoon paprika
- 1 teaspoon dried oregano
- Salt and pepper, to taste
- Fresh herbs (such as parsley or cilantro) for garnish
- Lemon wedges for serving

Instructions:

Preheat the grill to medium-high heat.

Rinse the fish fillets under cold water and pat them dry with paper towels.

In a small bowl, whisk together olive oil, lemon juice, minced garlic, paprika, dried oregano, salt, and pepper to create the marinade.

Place the fish fillets in a shallow dish or a resealable plastic bag. Pour the marinade over the fish, ensuring they are well-coated. Marinate for at least 15-30 minutes in the refrigerator.

Remove the fish from the refrigerator and let it come to room temperature for a few minutes.

Brush the grill grates with a bit of oil to prevent sticking. Place the fish fillets on the preheated grill.

Grill the fish for about 3-5 minutes per side, depending on the thickness of the fillets. Fish is done when it easily flakes with a fork.

While grilling, you can baste the fish with any remaining marinade to add more flavor.

Once the fish is cooked through and has a nice grill mark, transfer it to a serving platter.

Garnish with fresh herbs, such as parsley or cilantro, and serve with lemon wedges on the side.

Grilled fish is versatile and can be served with various side dishes like grilled vegetables, rice, or a fresh salad. Enjoy the simplicity and natural flavors of this Pescado a la Parilla dish!

Gambas a la Catalana (Catalan-Style Shrimp)

Ingredients:

- 1 pound large shrimp, peeled and deveined
- 2 tablespoons olive oil
- 4 cloves garlic, thinly sliced
- 1/2 teaspoon red pepper flakes (adjust to taste)
- 1 cup crushed tomatoes
- 1/4 cup dry white wine
- 1 teaspoon sweet paprika
- Salt and black pepper, to taste
- 2 tablespoons chopped fresh parsley
- Crusty bread for serving

Instructions:

Heat olive oil in a large skillet over medium heat.

Add sliced garlic and red pepper flakes to the skillet. Sauté for about 1-2 minutes until the garlic becomes fragrant but not browned.

Add the shrimp to the skillet, season with salt and black pepper, and cook for 2-3 minutes on each side until they start to turn pink and opaque.

Pour in the white wine and let it simmer for 1-2 minutes to reduce slightly.

Add the crushed tomatoes and sweet paprika to the skillet, stirring to combine.

Allow the sauce to simmer for an additional 5-7 minutes until the flavors meld and the shrimp are fully cooked.

Adjust the seasoning with salt and pepper to taste.

Sprinkle chopped fresh parsley over the dish and stir to combine.

Remove the skillet from heat and serve the Gambas a la Catalana hot, directly from the skillet.

Serve with crusty bread on the side to soak up the delicious sauce.

Enjoy this flavorful Catalan-style shrimp dish with its rich tomato and garlic sauce. It's perfect for a tapas-style meal or as a main course served over rice or pasta.

Espárragos a la Plancha (Grilled Asparagus)

Ingredients:

- 1 pound fresh asparagus spears, tough ends trimmed
- 2 tablespoons olive oil
- Salt and pepper, to taste
- Lemon wedges for serving (optional)

Instructions:

Preheat the grill to medium-high heat.
Rinse the asparagus spears under cold water and pat them dry with a paper towel.
In a large bowl, toss the asparagus with olive oil, ensuring that they are evenly coated.
Season the asparagus with salt and pepper to taste. You can also add other seasonings like garlic powder or lemon zest if desired.
Place the asparagus spears on the preheated grill, perpendicular to the grates to prevent them from falling through.
Grill the asparagus for 5-7 minutes, turning them occasionally to ensure even cooking. The asparagus should be tender and slightly charred.
Remove the grilled asparagus from the heat and transfer them to a serving platter.
Optionally, squeeze fresh lemon juice over the grilled asparagus or serve them with lemon wedges on the side for added brightness.
Serve the Espárragos a la Plancha hot as a side dish or appetizer.

Grilled asparagus makes a wonderful accompaniment to various dishes, such as grilled meats, seafood, or as part of a vegetable platter. It's a quick and tasty way to enjoy this nutritious and flavorful vegetable.

Tarta de Manzana (Spanish Apple Cake)

Ingredients:

- 4 large apples (peeled, cored, and sliced)
- 2 cups all-purpose flour
- 1 1/2 teaspoons baking powder
- 1/2 teaspoon baking soda
- 1/2 teaspoon salt
- 1 teaspoon ground cinnamon
- 1/2 teaspoon ground nutmeg
- 4 large eggs
- 1 cup granulated sugar
- 1 cup vegetable oil or melted butter
- 1 teaspoon vanilla extract
- Powdered sugar for dusting (optional)

Instructions:

Preheat your oven to 350°F (175°C). Grease and flour a round cake pan.
In a medium bowl, whisk together the flour, baking powder, baking soda, salt, ground cinnamon, and ground nutmeg. Set aside.
In a large mixing bowl, beat the eggs and sugar together until well combined and slightly pale.
Add the vegetable oil or melted butter to the egg mixture and continue beating until smooth.
Stir in the vanilla extract.
Gradually add the dry ingredients to the wet ingredients, mixing until just combined. Do not overmix.
Gently fold in the sliced apples until they are evenly distributed throughout the batter.
Pour the batter into the prepared cake pan, spreading it evenly.
Bake in the preheated oven for about 45-50 minutes, or until a toothpick inserted into the center comes out clean.
Allow the Tarta de Manzana to cool in the pan for about 15 minutes before transferring it to a wire rack to cool completely.
Once the cake has cooled, you can dust it with powdered sugar for a decorative touch.

Slice and serve the Spanish Apple Cake on its own or with a dollop of whipped cream or a scoop of vanilla ice cream, if desired.

Enjoy this delicious Tarta de Manzana, a perfect dessert for any occasion with its combination of moist cake and sweet, tender apples.

Conejo con Alioli (Rabbit with Garlic Mayo)

Ingredients:

For the Rabbit:

- 1 whole rabbit, cleaned and cut into serving pieces
- Salt and black pepper, to taste
- 3 tablespoons olive oil
- 1 onion, finely chopped
- 3 cloves garlic, minced
- 1 bay leaf
- 1 sprig of rosemary (optional)
- 1 cup white wine
- 1 cup chicken or rabbit broth (or water)

For the Alioli Sauce:

- 4 cloves garlic, minced
- 1 teaspoon Dijon mustard
- 2 egg yolks
- 1 cup extra-virgin olive oil
- Salt, to taste
- Lemon juice, to taste

Instructions:

Prepare the Rabbit:
- Season the rabbit pieces with salt and black pepper.
- In a large, deep skillet or Dutch oven, heat the olive oil over medium-high heat.
- Brown the rabbit pieces on all sides until they develop a golden crust.
- Add the chopped onion and minced garlic to the skillet. Sauté until the onions are translucent.

Cooking the Rabbit:
- Pour in the white wine and let it simmer for a few minutes, allowing the alcohol to evaporate.
- Add the bay leaf and rosemary (if using) to the skillet.
- Pour in the chicken or rabbit broth (or water).

- Reduce the heat to low, cover the skillet, and simmer for about 45 minutes to 1 hour or until the rabbit is tender. Add more liquid if needed during cooking.

Prepare the Alioli Sauce:
- In a mortar and pestle, combine minced garlic with a pinch of salt. Crush the garlic to form a smooth paste.
- Transfer the garlic paste to a bowl and add the Dijon mustard and egg yolks. Mix well.
- Gradually add the extra-virgin olive oil, whisking constantly to form a thick mayonnaise-like consistency.
- Season the alioli with salt and add lemon juice to taste.

Serve:
- Once the rabbit is cooked and tender, remove the bay leaf and rosemary sprig.
- Serve the rabbit pieces on a platter, drizzling the alioli sauce over the top.
- Garnish with chopped parsley if desired.

Enjoy Conejo con Alioli with crusty bread or your favorite side dishes. The rich and garlicky alioli sauce complements the tender rabbit, creating a delicious and hearty Spanish dish.

Garbanzos con Espinacas (Chickpeas with Spinach)

Ingredients:

- 2 cans (15 ounces each) chickpeas, drained and rinsed (or 3 cups cooked chickpeas)
- 2 tablespoons olive oil
- 1 onion, finely chopped
- 3 cloves garlic, minced
- 1 teaspoon smoked paprika
- 1 teaspoon ground cumin
- 1/2 teaspoon ground coriander
- 1/2 teaspoon cayenne pepper (optional, for heat)
- 1 can (14 ounces) diced tomatoes
- 1 bay leaf
- 1 cup vegetable broth
- Salt and black pepper, to taste
- 1 bunch fresh spinach, washed and chopped
- Lemon wedges, for serving

Instructions:

In a large pot or deep skillet, heat the olive oil over medium heat.
Add the chopped onion and sauté until it becomes translucent.
Add the minced garlic and sauté for an additional 1-2 minutes until fragrant.
Stir in the smoked paprika, ground cumin, ground coriander, and cayenne pepper (if using). Cook for another minute to toast the spices.
Pour in the diced tomatoes with their juices, stirring to combine.
Add the drained and rinsed chickpeas to the pot, along with the bay leaf.
Pour in the vegetable broth, season with salt and black pepper, and bring the mixture to a simmer.
Reduce the heat to low, cover the pot, and let it simmer for about 15-20 minutes to allow the flavors to meld.
Stir in the chopped spinach and cook for an additional 5-7 minutes, or until the spinach wilts and the chickpeas are heated through.
Adjust the seasoning with salt and pepper as needed.
Remove the bay leaf before serving.

Serve Garbanzos con Espinacas hot, either as a main dish or a side, with lemon wedges on the side for a refreshing touch.

Enjoy this nutritious and flavorful Spanish dish! It's perfect on its own, served over rice, or with a slice of crusty bread.

Caracoles a la Andaluza (Andalusian-Style Snails)

Ingredients:

- 2 pounds live snails (thoroughly cleaned and purged, if not already prepared)
- 1/2 cup olive oil
- 1 onion, finely chopped
- 4 cloves garlic, minced
- 1/2 cup dry white wine
- 1 bay leaf
- 1 teaspoon ground cumin
- 1 teaspoon sweet paprika
- 1/2 teaspoon cayenne pepper (adjust to taste)
- Salt and black pepper, to taste
- 1 cup chicken or vegetable broth
- 1/4 cup fresh parsley, chopped (for garnish)
- Crusty bread, for serving

Instructions:

If you're working with live snails, make sure they are thoroughly cleaned and purged. You can do this by placing them in a container with cornmeal or flour for a day, allowing them to expel any impurities.
In a large pot, heat the olive oil over medium heat.
Add the chopped onion and sauté until it becomes translucent.
Stir in the minced garlic and cook for an additional minute until fragrant.
Add the cleaned snails to the pot and cook for a few minutes, stirring to coat them in the aromatic mixture.
Pour in the white wine and let it simmer for a couple of minutes to allow the alcohol to evaporate.
Add the bay leaf, ground cumin, sweet paprika, cayenne pepper, salt, and black pepper. Stir to combine.
Pour in the chicken or vegetable broth, ensuring that the snails are partially submerged in the liquid.
Reduce the heat to low, cover the pot, and let the snails simmer for about 1 to 1.5 hours or until they are tender.
Check the seasoning and adjust salt and pepper as needed.
Once the snails are cooked, remove the bay leaf.

Serve Caracoles a la Andaluza hot, garnished with chopped parsley.
Provide crusty bread on the side to soak up the flavorful broth.

Enjoy Caracoles a la Andaluza as a unique and delicious culinary experience. Keep in mind that snails may not be readily available, so you might need to visit a specialty store or market to find them.

Pastel Vasco (Basque Cake)

Ingredients:

For the Pastry:

- 2 cups all-purpose flour
- 1 cup unsalted butter, cold and diced
- 1/2 cup granulated sugar
- 1 large egg
- Zest of 1 lemon
- 1/4 teaspoon salt

For the Almond Cream:

- 1 cup ground almonds
- 1 cup granulated sugar
- 1/2 cup unsalted butter, softened
- 2 large eggs
- 1 teaspoon almond extract
- 1 tablespoon all-purpose flour
- A pinch of salt

For the Egg Wash:

- 1 egg, beaten

Instructions:

For the Pastry:

In a large bowl, combine the flour, sugar, lemon zest, and salt.
Add the cold, diced butter to the flour mixture. Using your fingertips or a pastry cutter, work the butter into the flour until the mixture resembles coarse crumbs.
Add the egg and gently knead the dough until it comes together. Be careful not to overwork the dough.

Shape the dough into a disc, wrap it in plastic wrap, and refrigerate for at least 1 hour.

For the Almond Cream:

In a bowl, combine the ground almonds, sugar, softened butter, eggs, almond extract, flour, and a pinch of salt. Mix until well combined and smooth.

Assembling the Pastel Vasco:

Preheat your oven to 350°F (175°C). Grease and flour a tart or pie pan.
Roll out two-thirds of the chilled pastry on a floured surface to fit the bottom and sides of the prepared pan. Place the rolled-out dough in the pan and press it against the bottom and sides.
Spoon the almond cream evenly over the pastry in the pan.
Roll out the remaining one-third of the pastry and place it over the almond cream, sealing the edges with the bottom crust. Trim any excess dough.
Brush the top of the pastry with the beaten egg to create a golden finish.
Use a sharp knife to make a crosshatch pattern on the top of the cake.
Bake in the preheated oven for about 30-35 minutes or until the pastry is golden brown and the almond cream is set.
Allow the Pastel Vasco to cool before slicing.

Serve slices of this Basque Cake at room temperature. It's a delightful treat with a perfect balance of flaky pastry and rich almond cream. Enjoy!

Boquerones en Vinagre (Marinated Anchovies)

Ingredients:

- Fresh anchovies (quantity depends on preference or availability)
- White wine vinegar
- Extra-virgin olive oil
- 2-3 cloves garlic, finely minced
- Fresh parsley, finely chopped
- Salt, to taste

Instructions:

Clean and Prepare the Anchovies:
- Rinse the fresh anchovies under cold running water.
- Using a sharp knife, cut off the heads and tails of the anchovies.
- Make a small incision along the belly of each anchovy and carefully remove the bones, leaving the fillets intact.

Marinating the Anchovies:
- Place the cleaned anchovy fillets in a shallow dish or a non-reactive container.
- In a separate bowl, mix equal parts white wine vinegar and extra-virgin olive oil. The quantity depends on the number of anchovies; you'll need enough to cover them.
- Add the finely minced garlic, chopped fresh parsley, and a pinch of salt to the vinegar and oil mixture. Stir well to combine.
- Pour the marinade over the anchovies, ensuring they are fully submerged. If needed, add more vinegar and oil in equal parts.
- Cover the dish with plastic wrap and refrigerate for at least 24 hours. The longer you marinate, the more flavorful the anchovies will become.

Serving:
- After marinating, drain the excess liquid from the anchovies.
- Arrange the Boquerones en Vinagre on a serving dish.
- Optionally, drizzle a bit of extra-virgin olive oil over the top and sprinkle additional chopped parsley for garnish.
- Serve the marinated anchovies as a tapa or appetizer, accompanied by crusty bread or as part of a seafood platter.

Boquerones en Vinagre are a delightful and refreshing dish, often enjoyed in Spain as part of a tapas spread. The combination of vinegar, olive oil, garlic, and parsley infuses the anchovies with a bright and tangy flavor.